I. O. U.

AN APPROACH FOR LIFE CHANGING LIVING

by
Dr. John C Lofton III

Proudly Published in the USA by
Books to Believe In
17011 Lincoln Ave. #408
Parker, CO 80134

Phone: (303)-794-8888

Find us on Facebook at
www.facebook.com/Books2BelieveIn

Follow us on Twitter at
@books2believein

Visit us at
BooksToBelieveIn.com

Cover Design by:
Capri Brock

ISBN: 1535294949

Acknowledgements

I want to thank God for the ability to put thought on paper in a manner that people can understand. I am eternally grateful to my family; Gordon, Lofton, and Ross. I am humbled by my wife Lillian for her belief in the crazy ideas I may come up with. I thank my children, Antonio, Shunté, LaMara, and Laila for making the sacrifices of time without dad for one reason or another. I want to thank my daughter-in-law Katherine for making my son a better person and for being a great mother to my grandchildren Xavier, Malachi, and Liam. To my brothers Torrance and Kendrick, thank you for being brothers. Mom and dad, you are the two that brought me into the world. Thank you for being there. My parents come from very large families (26 brothers and sisters between the two of them), I want to thank all my aunts, uncles and cousins for making growing up so much fun. I love each of you but writing about each of you would be a book in itself. To Curtis and Flo; thank you for being an amazing father and mother in-law. To my little (short) big sis in-law, Tarica, you are always there; thank you. All of my nieces and nephews, this book is for you. You are the future of the world; develop to be the salt of the world.

Special thanks to my friends and anyone that contributed to this effort through statements, proofreading or motivation. I would also like to thank EJ Thorton, Capri Brock and their team at Books to Believe In for their belief and guidance through this process. This would not have been possible without your help.

Table of Contents

Prologue

It is very easy to be selfish. It is coded in our human make up so we are all susceptible. It is important that we understand this. Einstein said that understanding the nature of a problem gets you half way to the solution. This book is but one recommendation for developing a solution. It is not the only solution. It is one solution that provides you an opportunity to agree (enact the process) or disagree (keep the path you are on).

Understanding the critical role we play in problems and solutions is the true goal of this book. When we understand ourself (Inward), we can affect change (Outward), to make the world a better place (Upward). This understanding gives power to no longer be enslaved by the false "priorities" that create personal, spiritual, social and business crises. We achieve a freedom to be change agents for society.

I was told many years ago that I should consider writing. As a sophomore in high school, I shrugged that off because it sounded like too much work. I was right! This may never be a classic to anyone besides me but it was well worth the work. No one ever asks a failure how they failed. I will share that my failure was in not doing this earlier. If for no other reason than a sense of pride in sharing thoughts that I hope will make our world a better place.

So give this book a read and be prepared to view life a little bit differently. Each small bit counts. I hope you can find something in it to share with others because I am thankful that I have the opportunity to share it with you. Now pour yourself a warm drink, settle yourself and get comfortable so that you can discover "An Approach for Life Changing Living."

Starting
Inward

Humility paves the road to success. We have to be humble in our own hearts before we can shape or benefit from the experiences of those around us. A focus on morality is very beneficial since it can show how small you may be in the world yet how big your actions can be. Success in life depends largely on interactions with those around you. The best way to understand a person is to first understand ourself. We are able to control almost all aspects of life when we are able to understand and control ourselves. We should conduct self-reflections to look for the content that is within, but never become immobilized as we try to learn ourself. *Not that I speak from want; for I have learned to be content in whatever circumstances I am* (Philippians 4:11).

We may not have all that we want in life, but the things we do have are more than enough. There are many people that would trade places with you in a heartbeat for they desire more. Not that it should make us satisfied in our present state, but we must learn to be content with the things we have. Our selfishness sow seeds of discontent in our hearts that drives us to complain about our current state all the time. We act like the children of Israel when they complained to God. In the Bible, Paul said that he had to **LEARN** to be content. That means that it was a process but he got it! We have to recognize that being content does not mean that we stop progressing; it just means that we stop complaining during our progression. In other words, be content, but not immobilized; thank God for where we are, but keep moving forward.

One of the most important things we have is our faith. When we are not content and we complain, it's just like saying, "God, I don't trust you to make things better for me. So, I'm going to go my own way this time and get the things I want!" When we do that, we show our lack of faith; we step out of His will and ruin our progression. One thing I have learned from growing up in an old southern church is that God has a plan, but you have to seek Him to find it. That is why the words, *Seek ye first the Kingdom of God and his righteousness* (Matthew 6:33) are so powerful. The word righteousness means "right-ness" or to be "aligned" with God. When you are aligned with his plan, you can rest assure that your present state is not your end. God said that all these things will be added to you. One thing we miss is that when God says "added," something has to be there to be added upon. In a nutshell, we have to be content with the things we have, seek him and he will add to what we have! Simple; but not easy to do because we must get our eyes off others, forget our past, and recondition our self to be content with our present state and not complain. We have to stop complaining and comparing our situation to others or to our past accomplishments. Don't stop moving, just stop complaining!

RECALL NOTICE

The Maker of all human beings is recalling all units manufactured, regardless of make or year, due to a serious defect in the primary and central component of the heart. This is due to a malfunction in the original prototypes; code named Adam and Eve, resulting in the reproduction of the same defect in all subsequent units. This defect has been technically termed "Sub-Sequential Internal Non-Morality," or more commonly known as S.I.N. Symptoms include:

1. Loss of Direction
2. Foul Vocal Emissions
3. Amnesia of Origin
4. Lack of Peace and Joy
5. Selfish or Violent Behavior
6. Depression or Confusion in the Mental Component
7. Fearfulness
8. Idolatry
9. Rebellion
10. Excessive Drinking

The Manufacturer, who is neither liable nor at fault for this defect, is providing factory-authorized repairs and services free of charge to correct this S.I.N defect. The repair technician, Jesus, has most generously offered to bear the entire burden of the staggering cost of these repairs. There is no additional fee required. The number to call for repair in all areas is: P-R-A-Y-E-R. Once connected, please upload your burden of S.I.N through the REPENTANCE procedure. Next, download ATONEMENT from the repair technician, Jesus, into the heart component. No matter how big or small the S.I.N defect; Jesus will replace it with:

1. Love
2. Joy
3. Peace
4. Patience
5. Kindness
6. Goodness
7. Faithfulness
8. Gentleness
9. Self-control

Please see the operating manual, the B.I.B.L.E. (Basic Instructions Before Leaving Earth) for further details on the use of these fixes.

WARNING: Continuing to operate the human being unit **without** correction voids any manufacturer warranties, exposing the unit to dangers and problems too numerous to list and will result in the human unit being permanently impounded.

DANGER: The human being units not responding to this recall action will have to be scrapped in the furnace. The S.I.N defect will not be permitted to enter Heaven so as to prevent contamination of that facility.

P.S. Please assist where possible by notifying others of this important recall notice. You can also contact the Father at any time through "knee-mail."

The Family

Do you know that if we died tomorrow, the company that we work for could easily replace us in a matter of days? The family that we leave behind will feel the loss for the rest of their lives. So why pour more of ourselves into work than into our family? It does not seem to be a wise investment. Yet what we typically do in our society is say "Excuse me" when we bump into a stranger; we are very polite. We go out of our way and will even say goodbye to the stranger but at home; a different story. Oh! How we treat our loved ones, young and old. We get entrenched in whatever we are doing and fail to see the "loved" one standing near us. We turn and nearly knock them over only to yell, "Move out of the way!" The "loved" one moves but with a broken heart. We do not even realize how harsh we have spoken until we are in bed and God's small but infinite voice says (this is us thinking about the day's events), "While dealing with a stranger, common courtesy you use, but the family you love, you seem to abuse." Jobs and friends are temporary; family is forever. When you start inward, it is about putting things in the right priority.

BIG ROCKS

One day a time management expert was speaking to a group of business students. To drive home a point, he used an illustration that the students would never forget. He pulled out a one-gallon, wide-mouthed Mason jar and set it on a table in front of him. Then he produced about a dozen fist-sized rocks and carefully placed them, one at a time, into the jar. When the jar was filled to the top and no more rocks would fit inside, he asked, "Is this jar full?" Everyone in the class said, "Yes." He reached under the table and pulled out a bucket of gravel. Then he dumped some gravel in and shook the jar causing pieces of gravel to work themselves down into the spaces between the big rocks. Then, he asked the group once more, "Is the jar full?" By this time the class was onto him. "Probably not," one of them answered. "Good!" he replied. He reached under the table and brought out a bucket of sand. He started dumping the sand in and it went into all the spaces left between the rocks and the gravel. Once more he asked the question, "Is this jar full?" "No!" the class shouted. Once again, he said, "Good!" Then, he grabbed a pitcher of water and began to pour it in until the jar was filled to the brim. Then, he looked up at the class and asked, "What is the point of this illustration?" One eager beaver raised his hand and said, "The point is, no matter how full your schedule is, if you try really hard, you can always fit some more things into it!" "No," the speaker replied, "that's not the point. The truth this illustration teaches us is: If you don't put the big rocks in first, you'll never get them in at all." What are the "big rocks" in your life? Remember to put these BIG ROCKS in first or you'll never get them in at all.

Controversy & Animosity

With good comes bad. No one successful ever achieved their success without some challenges along the way. *Be not deceived; God is not mocked: for whatsoever a man soweth, that shall he also reap* (Galatians 6:7). To get we have to give. To rise we have to fall. There is a law built into the earth. It does not matter what race, religion, or background we are from; we will grow what we plant. When we sow it or plant it, we reap it. We always reap more than we sow. When people do us wrong and hurt us, let the law of reaping and sowing handle them. We do not have to say a word most times. Just let it work itself out. There is one very important thing we usually miss about the law of reaping and sowing. We forget that there is dirt involved!

When we sow or plant a seed, we surround it with dirt. Even though it is covered with dirt, fruit will grow out of it. That is the way God wants us. He allows us to be surrounded by dirt at times so we can grow out of it! The dirt that is going on around us, the dirt that has been shoveled on top of us, and the dirt that our past may have put into us will only grow us up and out! Fertilizer is the waste that passes out of the body of an animal. It is basically what Paul called, "DUNG!" To us, that is the most detestable thing, but it is needed for growing a seed. Any farmer will tell you that you grow better fruit when you use fertilizer; it is no different for us. We grow stronger and are made better when our lives have come through the dung. Once we pass through the mess, we are blessed! When we are in the mess, with the mess, and surrounded by the mess, that is the best time to sow a seed. We are in a fertile situation when you are covered with dirt and sprinkled with fertilizer! We are in the best possible position to grow and bring forth good fruit! So, when we are in the ground, covered with dirt, sow a seed of righteousness by reading the word; saying a prayer. Sow a seed of hope by praying for those that are taking you through. Don't look at the dirt as always being a bad thing. God uses dirt to grow us into what he wants us to be. Another thing that can be done from an internal perspective is to change the way we interpret and react to negativity when it occurs.

FOG &

FRICTION

A man hopped into a taxi on his way to the airport. The taxi cab driver was in the right lane when suddenly a black car jumped out of a parking space right in front of the taxi. The taxi driver slammed on his breaks, skidded, and missed the other car by just inches! The driver of the other car whipped his head around and started yelling at the taxi driver. The taxi driver just smiled and waved at the guy; he was really friendly. The passenger asked the taxi driver, "Why did you just do that? That guy almost ruined your car and sent us to the hospital!" The taxi driver answered with, "The Law of the Garbage Truck." He explained that many people are like garbage trucks. They run around full of garbage, full of frustration, full of anger, and full of disappointment. As their garbage piles up, they need a place to dump it and sometimes they will dump it on you. The taxi driver said, "Don't take it personally. Just smile, wave, wish them well, and move on. Don't take their garbage and spread it to other people at work, at home, or on the streets." What the taxi driver was saying is that successful people do not let garbage trucks take over their day.

Life is too short to wake up in the morning with regrets, so love the people who treat you right and pray for the ones who do not. Life is ten percent what you make it and ninety percent how you take it!

As we move through life, there will always be doubt. This is another part of human nature. Our challenge is to successfully recognize and address self-doubt. People around us will spread seeds of doubt at times. There is no reason for us to add to it.

GET OUT
OF YOUR WAY

You went to work and there was a big sign as you entered the door that stated, "Yesterday the person who has been hindering your growth passed away. We invite you to come to the auditorium to pay your final respects." As is typically the case, you as well as everyone in your office is sad due to the death of a colleague. However, after a while you start to question, who was it? Who was the person that had been hindering your growth? As you make your way to the auditorium, you see security controlling the crowd within the room. As people got close to the coffin and looked inside; they became speechless. They stood near the coffin, shocked and in silence, as if someone had touched the deepest part of their soul. There was a mirror inside the coffin: everyone who looked inside it could see their reflection. Next to the mirror was a message that said, "There is only one person who is capable of setting limits on your growth: it is YOU." Your life does not change when your boss changes, when your friends change, when your parents change, or even when your partner changes. Your life changes when YOU change, when you go beyond your limiting beliefs.

Internally Dealing with External Roadblocks

We can move our self out of our way but the truth of the matter is that we may also have to move others out our way; we call them naysayers. Did you know Nehemiah's team rebuilt the walls of Jerusalem with a sword in one hand and a trowel in the other? This understanding is significant because even though God gives us a plan, chances are we will have to fight to achieve the plan. Here's a sad truth, not everyone wants us to succeed. In fact, some will do everything they can to stop us. That is why we must constantly remind our self that God gave us the plan, that he is on our side, and that if we are willing to persevere; we will win. God guarantees it! Every minute devoted to our critics is time stolen from our God-given assignment. Do not step down to their level! It is not what our enemies say that matters; it is what we say to our self when our enemies get through talking. That is the way we nurture a winning attitude. We cannot leave crumbs.

We get out of a bad relationship, but we are still resentful and angry because we leave crumbs.

We get out of financial debt, but we still cannot control the desire to spend on frivolous things because we leave crumbs.

We get out of a bad habit or addiction, but we still long to try it just one more time because we leave crumbs.

We say, I forgive you, but we do not seem to forget or have peace with that person because we leave crumbs.

We tell our unequally yoked mate that it is over, but we still continue to call because we leave crumbs.

We get out of that horribly oppressive job, but we are still trying to sabotage the company after we left because we leave crumbs.

We cut off the affair with that married person, but we still lust after them because we leave crumbs.

We break off our relationship with that hurtful, abusive person, but we are suspicious and distrusting of every new person we meet because we leave crumbs.

We decide to let go of the past hurts from growing up in an unstable environment, yet we believe we are unworthy of love from others and refuse to get attached to anyone because we leave crumbs.

When we put the bags out we have to make sure we sweep the crumbs out as well! When we decide to address our self-doubt and the naysayers, it is inevitable that we will start to identify other areas where we can experience gains. In doing so, make the decision that once we make the change, we completely make the change. Making the change will require some determination.

DETERMINATION

Once upon a time there was a bunch of tiny frogs who arranged a running competition. The goal was to reach the top of the Eiffel Tower. A big crowd gathered to see the race once it began. The fact of the matter was that no one in crowd believed that any of the frogs would reach the top of the tower. Some of the thoughts that were verbally shared were, "**WAY** too difficult; they will **NEVER** make it to the top; not a chance that they will succeed; the tower is too high!"

As the race went on, the frogs began collapsing. There were some that kept a good tempo and climbed higher and higher. The crowd continued to yell, "It is too difficult! No one will make it!" More frogs got tired; more gave up but one continued to go higher and higher and higher; the frog would not give, up! The frog finally made it to the top. A contestant asked the frog how he had found the strength to succeed and reach the top of the Eiffel Tower. It turned out that the frog was deaf.

The point of this story is that you should never listen to other people's tendencies to be negative or pessimistic. It allows them to take your dreams and wishes away from you. You have to understand the power of words. Because everything you hear or read will affect your actions! ALWAYS be...POSITIVE! Above all; be deaf when people tell you that you cannot do something. Most people walk in and out of your life but positive people leave footprints in your heart. In two days tomorrow will be yesterday; to the world you might be one person but to one person you might be the world. If you fall down 10 times, Stand up 11.

Same Old Same Old

Therefore, since we are surrounded by such a huge crowd of witnesses to the life of faith, let us strip off every weight that slows us down, especially the sin that so easily hinders our progress. And let us run with endurance the race that God has set before us.

(Hebrews 12:1)

The devil has no new tricks. He keeps using the same things over and over to test us, try us, and cause us to fall. But God never lives in the past. How many times have you ever heard God say in His Word, "If you had done this, you would have this?" Never! God only moves forward. He doesn't even consider our past when he is working on us. As a matter of fact, he doesn't even care to remember our past. But the enemy keeps bringing situations that once caused us to stumble. When it involves our past, or when it's something that we once struggled with, you can bet it's the enemy testing our progress. God matures us, and then God allows the enemy to try us to prove our progress. Before we can move to the next level, we must first pass the test for the level we are on now. So many of us are stuck on the same level for years because we will not let go of people, places, or things, that cause us to fall. But until we master our level, we will not be promoted.

We have to desire to be better to get better, and we have to desire to be free to get free. As long as we are holding on to the same stuff, then we will not make any progress. God wants us to desire to please him and desire a better way of living. Sometimes we can do the same thing for so long that we lose sight of the real way it should be done. This is why church, fellowship, and reading the word is so important because it does not let us stay the same, but seeing others and hearing other testimonies and reading what God said will cause us to grow and not stay the same. Anything that does not grow is dead! Plain and simple, we will be walking as a spiritually dead person if we stop growing. So we have to strive for excellence in our walk and get hip to the devil's tactics. Know it is him and recognize when we should change things in our life. When that same old temptation comes, start resisting with everything you got! When that same old depression comes, block it out and speak the Word of God. When that same old situation tries to raise its head; run for your life into the shadow of the Almighty. Do what you have to do, but avoid doing the same old things.

There is only one corner of the universe you can be certain of improving and that is your own self.

– Aldous Huxley

Moving Outward

A good name is rather to be chosen than great riches.

(Proverbs 22:1)

Much of what has been shared to this point has addressed our own selfish nature: me, myself and I. That is not meant to be taken negatively because it is human nature to care about self. Self-preservation is a very strong motivating force that allows us to take care of "home" so that we can go out into the yard (the world) to do our gardening. When we know ourself completely (if we ever will) we can begin to understand others. To know others for more than face value, we should study their posture and the way they walk; the tone of their voice; their eyes; and their use of words. These avenues present a view into the real person. For deeper understanding, watch them when they are angry, in love, in trouble, learning of another's good fortune, learning of another's misfortune or trying to make a good impression on others. Watching a person through a number of moods or occasions allows us to understand the person through different lens because we have no right to judge others at sight. As we move beyond self and focus outward on others, we have to live with integrity and recognize that the challenges we may face will not be new. The passage from Proverbs addresses the importance of your name. If there is one thing you can protect in this world, it is your family name. Much of that protection resides in your integrity.

What do people think when they hear our name? Do they think, "Oh, that person is always so trustworthy and faithful; they always do the right thing?" Or do they think, "Watch out for that person. You never know what they're going to do?" We might say, "Oh, I'm a pretty good person. I do the right thing most of the time." We can veer off course just a little bit, and before we know it, we are miles away from our destination. Don't allow the little things to keep us from our destiny; choose integrity-even when no one is looking. For instance, when we need paper at home, don't take supplies from the office. Or, when we run into a store for a minute, don't park in the handicap parking spot unless you're supposed to. Sure, we might need a few extra bucks this week, but if the checkout clerk makes a mistake and gives back too much money, that is not God's provision; that's a test of integrity. If we will be faithful and choose integrity in the little things, it will be a great treasure in our life. God will pour out his blessing on us as we honor him all the days of our life.

ELECTION TRUTHS

While walking down the street one day a "Member of Congress" is tragically hit by a truck and dies. His soul arrives in heaven and is met by St. Peter at the Pearly Gates. "Welcome to heaven," says St. Peter. "Before you settle in, it seems there is a problem. We seldom see a high official around these parts, you see, so we're not sure what to do with you."

"No problem, just let me in," says the congressman.

"Well, I'd like to, but I have orders from higher up. What we'll do is have you spend one day in hell and one in heaven. Then you can choose where to spend eternity."

"Really, I've made up my mind. I want to be in heaven," says the Congressman.

"I'm sorry, but we have our rules." And with that, St. Peter escorts him to the elevator and he goes down, down, down to hell. The doors open and he finds himself in the middle of a green golf course. In the distance is a clubhouse and standing in front of it are all his friends and other politicians who had worked with him. Everyone is very happy and in evening dress. They run to greet him, shake his hand, and reminisce about the good times they had while getting rich at the expense of people. They play a friendly game of golf and then dine on lobster, caviar and champagne. Also present is the devil, who really is a very friendly and nice guy who has a good time dancing and telling jokes. They are having such a good time that before he realizes it, it is time to go. Everyone gives him a hearty farewell and waves while the elevator rises. The elevator goes up, up, up and the door reopens in heaven where St. Peter is waiting for him. "Now it's time to visit heaven."

24 hours pass with the Congressman joining a group of contented souls moving from cloud to cloud, playing the harp and singing. They have a good time and, before he realizes it, the 24 hours have gone by and St. Peter returns. "Well, then, you've spent a day in hell and another in heaven. Now choose your eternity."

The Congressman reflects for a minute, then he answers: "Well, I would never have said it before, I mean heaven has been delightful, but I think I would be better off in hell." So St. Peter escorts him to the elevator and he goes down, down, down to hell. The doors of the elevator open and he's in the middle of a barren land covered with waste and garbage. He sees all his friends, dressed in rags, picking up the trash and putting it in black bags as more trash falls from above. The devil comes over to him and puts his arm around his shoulder.

"I don't understand," stammers the Congressman. "Yesterday I was here and there was a golf course and clubhouse, and we ate lobster and caviar, drank champagne, and danced and had a great time. Now there's just a wasteland full of garbage and my friends look miserable. What happened?"

The devil looks at him, smiles and says, "Yesterday we were campaigning. Today you voted."

So, what do you value? I am an advocate of the fact that things will happen around you and things will happen to you but what is most important is what happens in you. We may never get everything right but that should not stop the effort.

To realize the value of a sister…Ask someone who doesn't have one.

To realize the value of ten years…Ask a newly divorced couple.

To realize the value of four years…Ask a graduate.

To realize the value of one year…Ask a student who has failed a final exam.

To realize the value of nine months…Ask a mother who gave birth to a stillborn.

To realize the value of one month…Ask a mother who has a premature baby.

To realize the value of one week…Ask an editor of a weekly newspaper.

To realize the value of one minute…Ask a person who has missed the train, bus or plane.

To realize the value of one-second…Ask a person who has survived an accident.

To realize the value of a friend or family member…LOSE ONE!

We have to hold tight to the ones we love because time waits for no one. We have to treasure every moment we have. You will treasure the moments even more when you can share it with someone special. We do not stumble upon the ones we love. I am not saying there is no such thing as love at first sight. That type of love is external. The type of love I am referring to is internal; a love that develops as we truly get to know someone and understand where their values may lay. Consider the lessons that can evolve out of the maybe.

MAYBE

Maybe…We were supposed to meet the wrong people before meeting each other so that when we finally meet the right person, we will recognize it and be grateful for that gift.

Maybe…It is true that we don't know what we have until we lose it, but it is also true that we don't know what we have been missing until it arrives.

Maybe…The happiest of people don't necessarily have the best of everything; they just make the most of everything they have.

Maybe…The brightest future will always be based on a forgotten past; don't trip on something right in front of you because you're looking behind you. You can't venture-on successfully in life, until you learn from and let go of your past mistakes, failures, and heartaches.

Maybe…Anything is possible with faith in your heart and GOD by your side. You should dream as if the possibilities are endless…because they are. The world is at your fingertips; just reach!!!

Maybe…You should never wait to tell someone how you feel about them, because one day it will be too late. Carpe Diem; I'd rather apologize for something I've said than be sorry that I never got the chance to say it.

Maybe…The best kind of friend is the kind whose presence is comforting and shielding. Someone you can sit by on a porch swing without saying a word, and still walk away feeling like you two just had the best conversation ever.

Maybe…Loving someone is giving them the ability to destroy your heart, and trusting them not to.

Maybe…Happiness awaits all those who cry, all those who hurt, all those who have lost, and for only they can truly appreciate the importance of all the people who have touched their lives.

Maybe…You shouldn't go for looks; they can deceive; don't go for wealth; even that fades away. Go for someone who makes you laugh. Laughter cures all ailments!! All it takes is a smile to make even the darkest day seem bright.

Maybe…You should hope for enough happiness to make you sweet, enough trials to make you strong, enough sorrow to keep you humble, and enough courage to keep you honest.

Maybe…You should try to live your life to the fullest because when you were born; you were crying and everyone around you was smiling, but when you die; you can be the one smiling and everyone around you is crying.

As we make our realizations and understand the world through the concept of maybe; we should stand firm in our understanding that some things can be quite definitive in shaping us as people. However, we have to develop one day at a time.

The most useless thing to do...Worry
The greatest Joy...Giving
The greatest loss...Loss of self-respect
The most satisfying work...Helping others
The ugliest personality trait...Selfishness
The most endangered species...Dedicated leaders
The greatest "shot in the arm"...Encouragement
The greatest problem to overcome...Fear
Most effective sleeping pill...Peace of mind
The most crippling failure disease...Excuses
The most powerful force in life...Love
The most dangerous pariah...A gossiper
The world's most incredible computer...The brain!
The worst thing to be without...Hope
The deadliest weapon...The tongue
The two most power-filled words..."I Can"
The greatest asset...Faith
The most worthless emotion...Self-pity
The most prized possession...Integrity
The most beautiful attire...A SMILE!
The most powerful channel of communication...Prayer
The most contagious spirit...Enthusiasm
The most important thing in life...GOD

It is better to be liked for the true you, than to be loved for who people think we are. That is one reason we should slow down and enjoy life and those around us. If we are happy inward, we should do our part to be an outward example for all to see. Point out and enjoy the natural highs of life.

John Lofton

NATURAL HIGHS

1. Falling in love.
2. Laughing so hard your face hurts.
3. A hot shower.
4. No lines at the supermarket
5. A special glance.
6. Getting mail.
7. Taking a drive on a pretty road.
8. Hearing your favorite song on the radio.
9. Lying in bed listening to the rain outside.
10. Hot towels fresh out of the dryer.
11. Chocolate milkshake (vanilla or strawberry).
12. A bubble bath.
13. Giggling.
14. The beach.
15. Finding a 20 dollar bill in your coat from last winter.
16. Laughing at yourself.
17. Looking into their eyes and knowing they love you.
18. Midnight phone calls that last for hours.
19. Running through sprinklers.

20. Laughing for absolutely no reason at all.

21. Having someone tell you that you're beautiful.

22. Laughing at an inside joke with FRIENDS

23. Accidentally overhearing someone say something nice about you.

24. Waking up and realizing you still have a few hours left to sleep.

25. Your first kiss (either the very first or with a new partner).

26. Making new friends or spending time with old ones.

27. Playing with a new puppy.

28. Having someone play with your hair.

29. Sweet dreams.

30. Hot chocolate.

31. Road trips with friends.

32. Swinging on swings.

33. Making eye contact with a cute stranger.

34. Making chocolate chip cookies.

35. Having your friends send you homemade cookies.

36. Holding hands with someone you care about.

37. Running into an old friend and realizing that some things (good or bad) never change.

38. Watching the expression on someone's face as they open a much desired present from you.

39. Watching the sunrise.

40. Getting out of bed every morning and being grateful for another beautiful day.

41. Knowing that somebody misses you.

42. Getting a hug from someone you care about deeply.
43. Knowing you've done the right thing, no matter what other people think.

Life is not a journey to the grave with the intention of arriving safely in a pretty and well preserved body, but rather to skid in broadside, thoroughly used up, totally worn out, and loudly proclaiming wow what a ride! Part of the great ride resides in the impact we have on others. There is a thought that if we have a life changing impact on those around us, when we die, we will never truly die. There are actually Bible verses that address our interaction with others.

The way you live will always honor and please the Lord, and you will continually do good, kind things for others. All the while, you will learn to know God better and better.

(Colossians 1:10)

Do for others what you would like them to do for you.

(Matthew 7:12)

I myself have gained much joy and comfort from your love, my brother, because your kindness has so often refreshed the hearts of God's people.

(Philemon 1:7)

Kindness is not a single act but a lifestyle. It is the habit of being helpful, encouraging, sympathetic, and giving - what we do for others that says, "I'm thinking of you." Even in confrontation, we can be kind. We practice kindness in all we do and say, always treating others as we would want to be treated. When we do that, we bring great refreshment to everyone we meet and we honor and please the Lord. Our kindness today may pass on to many generations and leave a lasting impression on more people than we realize. As we influence outward to have positive impact on those around us, we should not lose sight of the fact that genuine love can be shown through simple acts. It does not need to be a physical touch as many have come to define the essence of love.

God's Promise

Your own soul is nourished when you are kind.

(Proverbs 11:17)

Is kindness overrated? Why should I be kind to others? The bible provides an answer.

Be kind to each other, tenderhearted, forgiving one another, just as God through Christ has forgiven you.

(Ephesians 4:32)

Love is patient and kind.

(1 Corinthians 13:4)

When you are harvesting your crops and forget to bring in a bundle of grain from your field, don't go back to get it. Leave it for the foreigners, orphans, and widows. Then the Lord your God will bless you in all you do.

(Deuteronomy 24:19)

Kindness is an act of love, and after loving God, loving others is the next greatest command. A simple but profound truth is that God blesses us for acts of kindness in ways that are best for us. You may think that having more money would be a great blessing, but God may know that a close friendship, a deeper relationship with him, or victory over a bad habit may be more valuable. As our kindness toward others blesses them, we in turn will be blessed by God's kindness. We have to know that as we show kindness and love, there will be those that will try to bring us down. Misery loves company and people do not have a problem with being a crab in the bucket that pulls us down. We cannot control others; we can only try to influence while controlling our self.

Our
Challenge

*Never let loyalty and kindness get away from you! Wear them like
a necklace; write them deep within your heart.*

(Proverbs 3:3)

*Bless them that curse you, and pray for them which despitefully use
you.*

(Luke 6:28)

When Jesus tells us to bless those that curse us, he is not talking
about being a wimp and allowing people to run all over us. He is
telling us to not take vengeance upon them, but to pray for them.
You see, there is always something behind people's actions. There is
always an issue or a circumstance surrounding a person's negative
actions. People are genuinely good and love to be happy. That's the
way God made us. But the cares or issues of this life come to
squeeze out happiness and joy and cause people to react to the pain
they have experienced.

Always look past people's actions! This is what Jesus is saying. Now, I'm not an advocator of staying around and taking verbal, physical, or even emotional abuse from anyone. This is not what Jesus is saying. He is saying that when people do us wrong there is always something behind it. And the good part is that whenever a person does a child of God wrong, God said he would take care of them for us. So, we really don't have to confront the person and start a situation with them. All we have to do is give it to God and pray that he will straighten them out for us. Not harm them, but pray that whatever is behind their actions will be healed and brought to surface so they may deal with it. This is the action of blessing those that curse you. We have the power to curse them back but Jesus says, not to do that; tell him about it. When we need his grace and mercy, it will come to us the same way and we may escape the wrath of consequence for our own mistakes. As we move outwards to impact others, there will be challenges. There will also be pleasant times and people who look out for you. It does not matter what the person looks like on the outside; it is the inside that counts.

NO CHARGE
FOR LOVE

A farmer had some puppies he needed to sell. He painted a sign advertising the 4 pups and set about nailing it to a post on the edge of his yard. As he was driving the last nail into the post, he felt a tug on his overalls. He looked down into the eyes of little boy.

"Mister," he said, "I want to buy one of your puppies."

"Well," said the farmer, as he rubbed the sweat off the back of his neck, "These puppies come from fine parents and cost a good deal of money."

The boy dropped his head for a moment. Then reaching deep into his pocket, he pulled out a handful of change and held it up to the farmer. "I've got thirty-nine cents. Is that enough to take a look?"

"Sure," said the farmer. And with that he let out a whistle. "Here, Dolly!" he called. Out from the doghouse and down the ramp ran Dolly followed by four little balls of fur.

The little boy pressed his face against the chain link fence. His eyes danced with delight. As the dogs made their way to the fence, the little boy noticed something else stirring inside the doghouse. Slowly another little ball appeared; this one noticeably smaller. Down the ramp it slid. Then in a somewhat awkward manner, the little pup began hobbling toward the others, doing its best to catch up.

"I want that one," the little boy said, pointing to the runt.

The farmer knelt down at the boy's side and said, "Son, you don't want that puppy. He will never be able to run and play with you like these other dogs would."

With that the little boy stepped back from the fence, reached down, and began rolling up one leg of his trousers. In doing so he revealed a steel brace running down both sides of his leg attaching itself to a specially made shoe. Looking back up at the farmer, he said, "You see sir, I don't run too well myself, and he will need someone who understands."

With tears in his eyes, the farmer reached down and picked up the little pup. Holding it carefully he handed it to the little boy.

"How much?" asked the little boy.

"No charge," answered the farmer, "There's no charge for love."

The world is full of people who need someone who understands. We have to remember that if our presence doesn't make an impact, our absence won't make a difference. The Thessalonians were converted to Christ not only because of the words of Paul and his men but also because of the example of their lives. It is important to remember that the world is watching us as followers of Christ. We have been called to be the salt and light of the earth. Jesus admonished us to let our lights shine brightly before men so that they may praise God for our good works. God's intention is not to give us fame; that brings no glory to His name. A life worthy of imitation is one that is surrendered to be used as a tool in the hands of God, to display His awesome power and glory. What do people see when they see you? If someone walked in your shoes for 24 hours, what would they learn about Christ? Living a life worthy of imitation is to be mindful that we are representatives of Christ to those around us. We can only reflect what or who we are facing. We must focus our attention on Christ and imitate Him. Let our words, actions, and behavior emulate the One who calls us His ambassador. Our footprints on this journey and in life, should lead the world to our source, our focus, and our example; Jesus Christ.

NAILS IN THE FENCE

There once was a little boy who had a bad temper. His Father gave him a bag of nails and told him that every time he lost his temper, he must hammer a nail into the back of the fence. The first day the boy had driven 37 nails into the fence. Over the next few weeks, as he learned to control his anger, the number of nails hammered daily gradually dwindled down. He discovered it was easier to hold his temper than to drive those nails into the fence. Finally the day came when the boy didn't lose his temper at all. He told his father about it and the father suggested that the boy now pull out one nail for each day that he was able to hold his temper.

The days passed and the young boy was finally able to tell his father that all the nails were gone. The father took his son by the hand and led him to the fence. He said, "You have done well, my son, but look at the holes in the fence. The fence will never be the same. When you say things in anger, they leave a scar just like this one. You can put a knife in a man and draw it out. But it won't matter how many times you say I'm sorry, the wound will still be there. A verbal wound is as bad as a physical one."

For anyone reading this book that may have known me for a while, please forgive me if I have ever left a "hole" in your fence. For those that are getting to know me, I am much more knowledgeable about my actions than I was in my early years. However, I am not perfect and I ask that you forgive me if I ever put a "hole" in your fence. It will never be intentional but "holes" can develop without us actually trying to make them.

Follow my example, as I follow the example of Christ.

(1 Corinthians 11:1)

Going
Upward

Everyone has a desire to have a meaningful impact on others regardless of if it is admitted or not. People do good and bad deeds in the world to provide for a person or cause. We started our journey looking within ourselves for better understanding of what it is to be us. With that understanding, we spread our wings to be an outward manifestation for others. Now we move upwards to make life changing impact for us, others and the world. Where do we start to find an example of what it means to be completely acceptable of all so that we can make our world better?

A BABY'S HUG

We were the only family with children in the restaurant. I sat Erik in a high chair and noticed everyone was quietly sitting and talking. Suddenly, Erik squealed with glee and said, "Hi." He pounded his fat baby hands on the high chair tray. His eyes were crinkled in laughter and his mouth was bared in a toothless grin, as he wriggled and giggled with merriment. I looked around and saw the source of his merriment with a zipper at half-mast and his toes poking out of his shoe and his hair was uncombed and unwashed. His whiskers were too short to be called a beard. It was a man whose pants were baggy, his shirt was dirty, and his nose was varicose. We were too far from him to smell, but I was sure he smelled. His hands waved and flapped on loose wrists.

"Hi there, baby; hi there, big boy. I see ya, buster," the man said to Erik.

My husband and I exchanged looks, "What do we do?" Erik continued to laugh and answer, "Hi." Everyone in the restaurant noticed and looked at us and then at the man. The old geezer was creating a nuisance with my beautiful baby.

Our meal came and the man began shouting from across the room, "Do ya patty cake? Do you know peek-a-boo? Hey, look, he knows peek-a-boo."

Nobody thought the old man was cute. He was obviously drunk. My husband and I were embarrassed. We ate in silence; all except for Erik, who was running through his repertoire for the admiring skid-row bum, who in turn, reciprocated with his cute comments. We finally got through the meal and headed for the door. My husband went to pay the check and told me to meet him in the parking lot. The old man sat poised between me and the door. "Lord, just let me out of here before he speaks to me or Erik," I prayed. As I drew closer to the man, I turned my back trying to sidestep him and avoid any air he might be breathing. As I did, Erik leaned over my arm, reaching with both arms in a baby's "pick me-up" position.

Before I could stop him, Erik had propelled himself from my arms to the man.

Suddenly a very old smelly man and a very young baby consummated their love and kinship. Erik in an act of total trust, love, and submission laid his tiny head upon the man's ragged shoulder. The man's eyes closed, and I saw tears hover beneath his lashes. His aged hands full of grime, pain, and hard labor, cradled my baby's bottom and stroked his back. No two beings have ever loved so deeply for so short a time.

I stood awestruck. The old man rocked and cradled Erik in his arms and his eyes opened and set squarely on mine. He said in a firm commanding voice, "You take care of this baby."

Somehow I managed, "I will," from a throat that contained a stone.

He pried Erik from his chest, lovingly and longingly, as though he were in pain. I received my baby, and the man said, "God bless you, ma'am, you've given me my Christmas gift." I said nothing more than a muttered thanks. With Erik in my arms, I ran for the car. My husband was wondering why I was crying and holding Erik so tightly, and why I was saying, "My God, my God, forgive me."

I had just witnessed Christ's love shown through the innocence of a tiny child who saw no sin, who made no judgment; a child who saw a soul, and a mother who saw a suit of clothes. I was a Christian who was blind, holding a child who was not. I felt it was God asking, "Are you willing to share your son for a moment?" when He shared His for all eternity. The ragged old man, unwittingly, had reminded me, "To enter the Kingdom of God, we must become as little children."

Sometimes, it takes a child to remind us of what is really important. We must always remember who we are, where we came from and, most importantly, how we feel about others. The clothes on your back or the car that you drive or the house that you live in does not define you at all; it is how you treat your fellow man that identifies who you are. The ironic thing is that the story points to something that many of us know inherently. The challenge is in navigating our actions 180 degrees outside of what is accepted as the norm in our current society. The media, movies and stories glamorize the mistreatment of people. I choose to smile and be happy. I have had people ask or say to me, "How is it that you are always so happy? You have so much energy, and you never seem to get down." My secret is that I have learned there is little I can do in my life that will make me truly happy of my own doing. I have to depend on God to make me happy and to meet my needs. When a need arises in my life, I have to trust God to supply according to HIS riches. I have learned that most of the time I don't need half of what I think I do. He has never let me down. That is why I am happy. It is not any harder than that, it is that simple. Most people feel that a bigger house, a better paying job or a nicer car will make them happy. We can't depend on the physical to make us happy because it is always short lived. Only GOD in His infinite wisdom can provide eternal happiness. We just have to believe it and do it. Really trust God! I have a few guidelines that I live by as I travel my journey upwards and I would like to share them with you.

CHANGE YOUR WAYS

1. QUIT WORRYING: Life will deal you blows but don't worry. God is there to take all your burdens and carry them for you. Or do you just enjoy worrying over every little thing that comes your way?

2. PUT IT ON THE LIST: No, not YOUR list; put it on God's to-do-list. Let God be the one to take care of the problem. Truth be told, he takes care of a lot of things for you that you never even realize.

3. TRUST GOD: Once you've given your burdens to God, quit trying to take them back. Have the faith that He will take care of all your needs, your problems and your trials.

4. LEAVE IT ALONE: Don't wake up one morning and say, "Well, I'm feeling much stronger now, I think I can handle it from here." Why do you think you are feeling stronger now? It's simple. You gave God your burdens and he is taking care of them.

5. TALK TO GOD: He wants you to forget a lot of things. Forget what was making you crazy. Forget the worry but please, don't forget to talk to God -OFTEN! Prayer is simply you having a conversation with God.

6. HAVE FAITH: Have faith in God for he knows what he is doing.

7. SHARE: You were taught to share when you were only two years old. When did you forget? That rule still applies. Share with those who are less fortunate than you. Share your joy with those who need encouragement. Share your laughter with those who haven't heard any in such a long time. Share your tears with those who have forgotten how to cry. Share your faith with those who have none.

8. BE PATIENT: You grow from a child to an adult, have children, change jobs many times, learn many trades, travel to so many places, meet thousands of people, and experience so much. How can you be so impatient then when it takes God a little longer than you expect to handle something on His to-do-list? Just because He created the entire universe in six days, everyone thinks He should always rush, rush, rush.

9. BE KIND: Be kind to others. They may not dress like you, or talk like you, or live the same way you do, but God created each of us different in some way. It would be too boring if we were all identical.

10. LOVE YOURSELF: As much as God loves you, how can you not love yourself?

HOT CHOCOLATE

A group of graduates, well established in their careers, were talking at a reunion and decided to go visit their old university professor. During their visit, the conversation turned to complaints about stress in their work and lives. Offering his guests hot chocolate, the professor went into the kitchen and returned with a large pot of hot chocolate and an assortment of cups - porcelain, glass, crystal, some plain looking, some expensive, some exquisite - telling them to help themselves to the hot chocolate.

When they all had a cup of hot chocolate in hand, the professor said: "Notice that all the nice looking expensive cups were taken, leaving behind the plain and cheap ones. While it is normal for you to want only the best for yourselves, that is the source of your problems and stress. The cup that you're drinking from adds nothing to the quality of the hot chocolate. In most cases it is just more expensive and in some cases even hides what we drink. What all of you really wanted was hot chocolate, not the cup; but you consciously went for the best cups and then you began eyeing each other's cups."

Now consider this: Life is the hot chocolate; your job, money and position in society are the cups. They are just tools to hold and contain life. The cup you have does not define, nor change the quality of what life is. Sometimes, by concentrating only on the cup, we fail to enjoy the hot chocolate God has provided us. God makes the hot chocolate, man chooses the cups.

The happiest people don't have the best of everything. They just make the best of everything that they have. Live simply; love generously; care deeply and speak kindly because it helps you enjoy your hot chocolate. By doing so, you position yourself to make a difference and move the world upward. This position is supported in the Bible through the story of Noah. The story teaches us:

1. ***You can make a difference in your family***. By faith Noah…built an ark to save his family. Noah's decision didn't just benefit him personally, it saved his entire household. It took many years, but he did it. By God's Grace you can win your family and others to Christ as well.

2. ***You can make a difference for future generations.*** Noah not only survived the flood, but God used him to start the world all over again. *The eyes of the Lord search the whole earth in order to strengthen those whose hearts are fully committed to Him* (2 Chronicles 16:9). God is looking for people who will partner with Him in fulfilling His purposes in the earth. But to qualify:

A. You must be willing to stand out in the crowd. Noah believed in his vision when nobody else did. Difference-makers are different; don't let that bother you.

B. You must not be afraid to do something for the first time. Don't let the words, "It's never been done before," keep you from obeying God. People probably told Noah, "It's never raining. Who needs a boat?" But they were wrong and Noah was right.

C. You must endure the rain in order to see the rainbow. *So take your stand and believe God, for what He has promised He will perform* (Jeremiah 1:12).

3. ***You can make a difference at any age***. Stop putting yourself down because of your age. Noah was five hundred years old when he started preaching and building the ark. It's not over until God says it's over!

We all may not have a Noah type of story. Many of us will be the person on the baseball or softball team that consistently gets the base hit. If sports is not something you can relate to, some of us will be musical one hit wonders but that one song can be a life changing event. In a world that celebrates bigger and better, how do you handle obscurity? Do you chafe under it? Do you secretly resent people further up the line? Before you answer, consider that there was only one Moses whose amazing life covered four Old Testament books; only one Paul who was called to write half the New Testament. The rest of us have been called to live further down the line, but each of us is important. Our valuables don't make us more valuable, and our net worth is not the basis of our self-worth. Our value was established at the cross. When others overlook us, we have to stop and remind our self that God values us so highly that He thought we were worth dying for.

Have you heard about the one-note musician? She inspected her violin, took her seat in the orchestra, arranged her music and tuned up her instrument. As the concert proceeded, the conductor cued one group of musicians after another until finally the crucial moment arrived. It was time for her one note to be played! The conductor signaled, she sounded her note - and the moment was over. Just like that! The orchestra played on and the one-note player sat there quietly for the rest of the concert; not disappointed that she'd played only one note, but with a sense of fulfilment that she'd played it in tune, on time, and with great gusto! Have you heard of Ananias? He shows up only one time in the Bible, leads Saul of Tarsus to Christ, then promptly exits (Acts 9:10-19). He's a one-note player - but what a note! We need to take our cue from him!

In understanding that all we do is through God, we are able to guide our upward journey by recognizing that many people will walk in and out of our life. But only true friends will leave footprints on our heart. We have to hold ourselves accountable to a few life facts and actions that continue to move us upward.

> To handle yourself, use your head; to handle others, use your heart.

Anger is only one letter short of danger.

If someone betrays you once, it is his fault; If he betrays you twice, it is your fault.

Great minds discuss ideas; Average minds discuss events; Small minds discuss people.

He, who loses money, loses much; He, who loses a friend, loses much more; He, who loses faith, loses all.

Beautiful young people are accidents of nature.

Learn from the mistakes of others. You can't live long enough to make them all yourself.

I have focused on smiling and being happy in this chapter. It was not by accident because moving upwards is something that happens with others. There is a saying that you get more bees with honey than you would with vinegar. Be happy and smile, it attracts people. Laugh; it exercises the muscles that are required to smile.

EXERCISING IN LAUGHTER

1. Recently, when I went to McDonald's, I saw on the menu that you could have an order of 6, 9 or 12 Chicken McNuggets. I asked for a half dozen nuggets. "We don't have half dozen nuggets," said the teenager at the counter. "You don't?" I replied. "We only have six, nine, or twelve," was the reply "So I can't order a half dozen nuggets, but I can order six?" "That's right." So I shook my head and ordered six McNuggets.

2. I was checking out at the local Wal-Mart with just a few items and the lady behind me put her things on the belt close to mine. I picked up one of those "divider" that they keep by the cash register and placed it between our things so they wouldn't get mixed. After the girl had scanned all of my items, she picked up the "divider", looking it all over for the bar code so she could scan it. Not finding the bar code she said to me, "Do you know how much this is?" I said to her "I've

changed my mind; I don't think I'll buy that today." She said "OK," and I paid her for the things and left. She had no clue to what had just happened.

3. A lady at work was seen putting a credit card into her floppy drive and pulling it out very quickly. When I inquired as to what she was doing, she said she was shopping on the Internet and they kept asking for a credit card number, so she was using the ATM thingy.

4. I recently saw a distraught young lady weeping beside her car. "Do you need some help?" I asked. She replied, "I knew I should have replaced the battery to this remote door unlocker. Now I can't get into my car. Do you think they (pointing to a distant convenience store) would have a battery to fit this?" "Hmm, I dunno. Do you have an alarm, too?" I asked. "No, just this remote thingy," she answered, handing it and the car keys to me. As I took the key and manually unlocked the door, I replied, "Why don't you drive over there and check about the batteries. It's a long walk."

5. Several years ago, we had an Intern who was none too swift. One day she was typing and turned to a secretary and said, "I'm almost out of typing paper. What do I do?" "Just use copier machine paper," the secretary told her. With that, the intern took her last remaining blank piece of paper, put it on the photocopier and proceeded to make five "blank" copies.

6. I was in a car dealership a while ago, when a large motor home was towed into the garage. The front of the vehicle was in dire need of repair and the whole thing generally looked like an extra in "Twister." I asked the manager what had happened. He told me that the driver had set the cruise control and then went in the back to make a sandwich.

7. My neighbor works in the operations department in the central office of a large bank. Employees in the field call him when they have problems with their computers. One night he got a call from a woman in one of the branch banks who had this question: "I've got smoke coming from the back of my terminal. Do you guys have a fire downtown?"

8. Police in Radnor, Pa. interrogated a suspect by placing a metal colander on his head and connecting it with wires to a photocopy machine. The message "He's lying" was placed in the copier, and police pressed the copy button each time they thought the suspect wasn't telling the truth. Believing the "lie detector" was working, the suspect confessed.

9. A mother calls 911 very worried asking the dispatcher if she needs to take her kid to the emergency room, the kid was eating ants. The dispatcher tells her to give the kid some Benadryl and it should be fine. The mother says, "I just gave him some ant killer!" Dispatcher: Rush him to emergency room!

We have to love our children. They are the reason we make our upward journey; to make the world better for them. However, in all their innocence, they can be funny as well.

A CHILD'S BOOK REPORT ON THE BIBLE

A child was told to write a book report on the entire Bible. Through the eyes of a child...Children's Bible in a Nutshell:

In the beginning, which occurred near the start, there was nothing but God, darkness, and some gas. The Bible says, "The Lord thy God is one," but I think he must be a lot older than that. Anyway, God said, "Give me a light!" and someone did. Then God made the world. He split the Adam and made Eve. Adam and Eve were naked, but they were not embarrassed because mirrors hadn't been invented yet. Adam and Eve disobeyed God by eating one bad apple, so they were driven from the Garden of Eden. Not sure where they were driven though, because they didn't have cars. Adam and Eve had a son, Cain, who hated his brother as long as he was Abel. Pretty soon all of the early people died off, except for Methuselah, who lived to be like a million or something.

One of the next important people was Noah, who was a good guy, but one of his kids was kind of a Ham. Noah built a large boat and put his family and some animals on it. He asked some other people to join him, but they said they would have to take a rain check. After Noah, came Abraham, Isaac and Jacob. Jacob was more famous than his brother, Esau, because Esau sold Jacob his birthmark in exchange for some pot roast. Jacob had a son named Joseph who wore a really loud sport coat.

Another important Bible guy is Moses, whose real name was Charlton Heston. Moses led the Israel Lights out of Egypt and away from the evil Pharaoh after God sent ten plagues on Pharaoh's people. These plagues included frogs, mice, lice, bowels, and no cable. God fed the Israel Lights every day with manicotti. Then he gave them His Top Ten Commandments. These include don't lie, cheat, smoke, dance, or covet your neighbor's stuff. Oh, yeah, I just thought of one more: Humor thy father and thy mother.

One of Moses' best helpers was Joshua who was the first Bible guy to use spies. Joshua fought the battle of Geritol and the fence fell over on the town. After Joshua, came David. He got to be king by killing a giant with a slingshot. He had a son named Solomon who had about 300 wives and 500 porcupines. My teacher says he was wise, but that doesn't sound very wise to me.

After Solomon, there were a bunch of major league prophets. One of these was Jonah, who was swallowed by a big whale and then barfed upon the shore. There were also some minor league prophets, but I guess we don't have to worry about them.

After the Old Testament came the New Testament. Jesus is the star of the New Testament. He was born in Bethlehem in a barn. (I wish I had been born in a barn, too, because my mom is always saying to me, "Close the door! Were you born in a barn!?" It would be nice to say, "As a matter of fact, I was.") During His life, Jesus had many arguments with sinners like Pharisees and the Republicans. Jesus also had twelve opossums, the worst one was Judas Asparagus. Judas was so evil that they named a terrible vegetable after him. Jesus was a great man. He healed many leopards and even preached to some Germans on the Mount. But the Republicans and all those guys put Jesus on trial before Pontius the Pilot. Pilot didn't stick up for Jesus. He just washed his hands instead. Anyways, Jesus died for our sins and came back to life again. He went up to Heaven but will be back at the end of the Aluminum. His return is foretold in the book of Revolution.

This book has been a collection of thoughts, stories, quotes and biblical lessons that have shaped the life of this country boy from Alabama. I pray that something in it will touch you in some way.

Epilogue

So what have you discovered? You have seen how knowing your self is the first step in touching and shaping others for a better world. God wants us to be more like Jesus Christ. To do that, we have to experience a change of heart. It starts within us.

You should never have to be a victim of circumstances again because you are the agent of change and that gives you freedom no matter the circumstances. You have discovered the power you have always had to change yourself, your environment and those around you. Your discovery can now change the world by empowering those around you.

Inward, Outward, Upward: An Approach for Life Changing Living.

About the Author

John C. Lofton III has been an organizational leader in the domestic and international environment for over 25 years. He has personally trained more than 100,000 leaders worldwide on the dynamics and rewards of leading in a changing environment. Dr. Lofton has spoken to leaders and organizations on the global stage and is an active professor providing instruction to future leaders in the areas of leadership, management and organizational behavior.

Bibliography

Allaway, A. & Allaway, D. *E-Praise 4 Gifting Christian E-mail Devotions*. ISBN 978-0-6151-6362-8 www.allaway books.com 2007

Allen, J. *As A Man Thinketh*. Hallmark Cards, Kansas City, 1968

Baker, D. & Baker, S. *101 Stories With Life-changing Lessons*. Oakwood University Publishing Office. Alabama, 2008

Bracken, T. *Could it Be that Simple?* Xulon Press. 2007

Covey, S. R. *Seven Habits of Highly Effective People*. Simon & Schuster. New York, 1989

Election Truths. (August 7, 2008). Retrieved from *http://www. americasdebate.com/forums/simple/index.php/t9566-450.html*

"Faith Fellowship Baptist Church." *www.faith-baptist aurora.org/ Sermons/Sermon_2003_05_04_FFBCA.pdf*. May 4, 2003

Frankl, V. E. *Man's Search For Meaning*. Washington Square Press. New York, 1985

ImNoBetterThanU. (April 5, 2008). Retrieved from *www.imno betterthanu.com/2008_04_01_archive.html*

Marsh, T. (July 20, 1998). Courting Business: A little free advice for self-employed. Retrieved from _http://web.kitsapsun.com/archive/1998/0720/0001_courting_business__a_little_free_.html_

Maybe. (August 2008). Retrieved from _http://www.atimetolaugh.org/directory-take-the__long-view.html#sthash.hvzXfHQW.dpbs_

Miller, M. _Mouse Attack 5!!! (The Final Cheese): A Collection of Emails._ Xilibris Corporation. 2010

Nails in the Fence. (July 1997). Retrieved from _http://www.inspirationpeak.com/cgi-bin/stories.cgi?record=50_ July 1997

Stalker, E. (2011). "On the North River" Retrieved from _http://onthenorthriver.com/2015/07/22/guest-old-folks/_

The Holy Bible

Virtue First Foundation. "Hot Chocolate." Retrieved from _http://www.virtuefirst.org/virtues/thankfulness/_

If you liked

I. O. U.
AN APPROACH FOR LIFE CHANGING LIVING

Please leave a review on
Amazon.com

Also available in Kindle

Made in United States
Troutdale, OR
08/08/2023

11900177R10044